The Dark Lords Message Inside A Bottle

The Lost Letters From Satan

By: Curtis Bridges

Supported By The Dark Lords Satanic Group
&
The New Mexico Satanist Group

A Quote From The Author

First off I would like to say thank you for buying my satanic book, I hope this book gives you a sense of relief from other satanic books, I want to flood the satanic community with my new satanic book writings, and you as the reader or the viewer can be open to something fresh and original, I'm vary close to the dark lord and he tells me things in my dreams & visions, that I received from him, I will testified to you that satan is really real, and that we must believe in the beloved dark father,

In my new satanic book the dark lords message inside a bottle, is satan lost messages to us, these were documents lost over period of time, and still never found today, this will give you a complete insight on what satan is really about, and how his plan of salvation has made us the way we are, satan is the key to happiness and a key to the way of life, never give up on satan, always believe in him, and believe in his plan of salvation,

I leave this message with you, that once you read my new book and testified to yourself that this book is the real document of satan, I promise satan will rewarded you and rewarded your life? hail Satan

Message From The Author Curtis Bridges, And Supported By a The Dark Lords Satanic Group & The New Mexico Satanist Group??

In the beginning of man & women, There was only one place to be at, And that was Heaven, Heaven was a place of salvation, and caring and loving place, It was a place to be at, But when Satan fell and lost the war, he was sent down here on earth, were he would become the new king of this place, Satan has two kingdoms, One is Hell & And the other one is Earth, Being on earth is a place were we have to see if we are a true loyal servant to lord satan, He challenges us every day to stay true to him,

One day satan made his bible, and it was a satanic bible that spoke the truth of satan, and it went into details on how satan was the beloved dark father, But this was a time that nobody believed in satan, and that satan grew vary weak & and upset, So one day satan goes to a island on earth, a place were he could think and relax at, satan told himself on how he could have loyal servants and to have people follow him. So satan kept on walking around the island and had a idea that struck him like lighting, Satan had a idea to write messages in a bottle and let the sea take these bottles to other places and this would be the way he would get loyal supporters from, so satan went back to his kingdom and goes about writing these letters, and to gain more loyal supporters,

But satan knew he had to be secretive about this, and that he didn't want these messages to fall in the wrong hands, he need to figure out on how he would keep this safe, and it hit him, he thought he would put the message inside a glass bottle, but only his loyal servants to satan could only open the bottle up and nobody else, only people that follow satan path?

Page 1

The Letter's Of Satan, And What He spoke Inside The Letters

Letter 1:

I say on to you, my loyal servants that I'm lord satan and king of the earth & hell, and I command you all to stay loyal to me, and to help build my army of darkness, We need your support and to help create a legion, Were we will all be happy at, I'm your beloved dark father and I love all of you and keep me close to your heart, My plan of salvation is true and that my kingdom is true, If any man Or women follows me and gives me your loyal support, I shall rewarded you & your family, And to received the full blessing of satan, I shall Give you life, Honor, Rsspect, Love, And children's. I shall give you everything you so desire,

I testified to you all that I'm the real and only god that loves you, and wants to see you prevail on earth?

Sign: Sincerely Satan

letter 2:

If anyone so desire to follow in my footsteps, and to become a leader for me, and that to speak the truth about my gospel, You shall be the one for me, any man that stand with me, and stands for who I am, shall become the leader, I shall give you children's to keep this process going for a long time, I'm Satan your lord & master, I command you all to stay true to what you believe In me, I shall give you a bible, that will testified to you all that this is the only true doctrine about me, Keep this bible true and to read it everyday to follow by, This bible is for you and for you to teach my gospel every single day, My bible is the key to me and to my kingdom, I shall give you a bible to raise the hell from beneath you and to give it upon you and your family, And Your Brother & Sister, And To All The Satanic Followers, This Is Your Bible?

Sign: Sincerely The Beloved Dark Father Lucifer

Page 2, The Letters From Satan

Letter 3:

Brothers & Sisters, And To All My Servants & Followers, I say on to you, that we must stick together and to form a alliance with other satanic groups to become one, we must fight for what we believe is to be true, I gave you a bible, to follow and to gospel about, and that the bible was your study guide to become the best follower you could be, now you know the bible, and I command you to go out and find other followers so they can preach my gospel and to build a church in my honor, once you build the church in my honor, I shall reign over it and to protect it, and to love it, My church is a place to worship me and to come together and speak the truth about me, No one that is my follower should never set a foot inside my church unless he's a person that wants to investigate my church to join,

Sign : Sincerely Lord Satan

letter 4

Once you completed my church, you shall take a handful of members and spread about the land teaching my gospel and to help other members out when needed, heal the sick in my name as satan, heal the wounded people in my name satan, preach to the homeless the word of satan, And Heal the Sick & The Dying in my name as satan, Once this is done you shall have your followers and loyal servants to keep building my church, I want my church's to be everywhere, so people can enjoy my gifts that I bring them, May they never forget me and my name?

Sign: Sincerely Lord Satan

Letter: 5

Once you completed my task that I ask for, your next step is to baptize the members in my name, and that the baptism is my protection over them, it's my love that I will show over you, it's a baptism to wash you away from the Christians bullshit that has reign over you, it's time to be baptize by your beloved dark father and become a faithful servant in my church, received my blessing, received my demons spirits around you, and to guide you, once the baptism is complete you will be mine faithful servant, and I shall rewarded you and give you what you desire,

Sign: Sincerely Lord Satan

Page 3, The Letters

letter: 6

Once baptize in my church, you should think about marriage and starting a family in my name, once this is done, I shall rewarded you and your family, your children will grow up to be loyal servants, and to be the next generation of loyal satanist, we must keep this alive, so it will never die out, give me what I ask for and you shall have what you desire in return, a satanic marriage is three things and that is you, your mate and satan, keeping satan in your marriage will help your marriage grow into something beautiful and remarkable, I shall give you everything you want, and in return be my loyal servant,

Sign: Sincerely Satan

Letter 7:

We must have rules & laws setup for the followers and members, this is a great way to stay protected by me and to protect yourself, we need these rules & laws in place so we can lived a better life, and to stay true to me as your supreme ruler and master, without these rules and laws we wouldn't know what to do for ourselves, and we will be lost forever, we must replace the old rules with new rules and to speak the truth, keeping these rules & laws close to your heart and live by them everyday, you will see a change in your life, and everything will fit into place, if you stand by me and trust to what you have to say, I promise you will have a place in my kingdom, I will make you a lord and a god in my kingdom, let us figure out on the new satanic rules for earth and the new satanic laws,

Sign: Sincerely Satan,

Page 4, The Letters

Letter 8:

To my fellow satanist and followers of me, I'm your lord and master and I shall build our legion ten fold, I shall give everything to man & women so they can survive the Christian bullshit and there lies, believe in me as the only god and ruler, and I shall give you something in return for being loyal, I will give you true happiness and riches in your life, we must build my empire up and be the supreme being on this earth, I command all of you to gather what you can and take up my gospel and seek out the true followers, so we can host there talents into what we need, I say onto you all, that we will survive this ordeal again and this time we will win the battle & war,

Sign: Beloved Dark Father Satan

Letter 9:

I say onto man that live by the rules that I have in place for you and you shall be a king and a warrior, I say unto women that give birth and create children to keep this legion going, and to stand by your mate and to protect each other from harms way, give me what I ask for and I shall give you the greatest gift know to man & women, never forget what I did for you and I'm the loving father, I shall give you everything, never give up on me and I shall never give up on you, Im the master and ruler of earth and I shall not have my legions fall to Christians and there gospel. Rewarded yourself and I shall taken upon you to be the highest of all holy,

Sign: Lord Satan

Page 5, The Letters

Letters To Satan

Letter 1:

Beloved dark lord, this is your loyal servant john, and I shall do what you command me to do, I shall build you a church and spread all of your churches nation wide and people should know your gospel, I shall gather all the members and to create new members, I shall grow your gospel in all the lands my dark lord, I shall stay your loyal servant until the end of time, nobody will stop me for doing my task, I shall ask you my dark lord once everything is completed, what shall I do next for you, what will you command me to do, I shall leave you this message by saying it's going to be a pleasure on doing this task and seeing everything fit into place, Hail Satan,

Sign: loyal Servant John

Letter 2:

Beloved dark father, we are taking enemy fire by one of the new churches that has been built in your name, the Christians army is strong and powerful and we are being cut off, I ask for your help and guidance and to ask for your protection, what shall we do my master, what can you do for us? We are low on supplies and weapons, I need re-forcement at once my lord, I hope you get this message and help us in the need of time, this will be my last message if we fail, Hail Satan

Sign: loyal Servant/ Sgt. Bitter men

Letter 3:

To the beloved dark father, I have gather about 200+ plus loyal servant to command your army! and to praise you every single day once you return to earth! I have found that we have reach the top of saying your gospel to other people and to other members! and they enjoyed on what we had to offer! you are the one true god and the only god for us! you are our beloved dark father and by the time this letters reach you! I would have about 1,000 strong loyal servants at your command my lord, we will pray in your name and shall wait to see you once more, Hail Satan

Sign: Loyal Servant Michael

Page 6, Letters To Satan

The letters that you heard from satan and his loyal servants, this was a way the communicated back in these days, by writing a letter and putting it in inside a bottle and sending it off Into the sea, these were the lost letters that was never recover but people say that the letters were in hiding, I've heard stories all my life that satan has lost valuable letters & scrolls up on this earth, but was never recover, but I believe that they were recover and put into hiding so no one would ever see them again. Satan has told me many of times in my dreams, that he has walked this whole earth but hasn't found his lost letters, let me show you on what he told his loyal servants in a letter that was wrote by satan, and you can see how much the anger he had inside of him,

Letter: 1

To my loyal servants, I'm writing you this letter to say that I'm vary displeased with each and everyone of you, for not finding my letters, and that they haven't been recover yet, I want to know why we haven't found my letters yet, and that do we know who took them or who's hiding them from us, I want to believe in each and everyone of you but my judgement is becoming cloudy really fast, we must find these letters fast, so it won't fall into the wrong hands, if it falls into such hands we could be lost forever, and I don't want to see this happen. I took so long to build this kingdom up, and I will not see it fall down, please keep me in the loop and progress you made on finding my letters,

Sign: The Dark Lord

Now in this letter I showed you, satan has grown vary angry and vary upset towards his followers for not finding his lost letters, and that they would be seeing satan angry for a vary long time to come, unless they found his letters and then they would of been rewarded and satan would love them for it, but many years past and still no recovery of satan letters and all the servants walked this whole earth but couldn't find it, there were rumors about the followers that someone took the letters for keep sake and hidden the letters so that it could never be found ever again,

Page 7

Many rumors has gone by, but none of them seem to be true, and that the loyal servants basically gave up and went there own ways, many of the followers did stay on board to find the lost letters of satan, but many just got up and left, Satan was still vary angry at his followers and the ones that got up and left satan could not come back to his kingdom, but had to stay on earth until there passing, Satan was hopeing that when he said that to the lost followers that they would rejoin into the search, but it didn't work. Many people got on with there lives and started a family, and told stories to there children about the lost letters, so the children would have something to do, kinda like finding buried treasure, Many people forgotten about the lost letters, most people thought it was a myth or something that could not been found ever again, I say people gave up to easily on the search of the lost letters,

And that the followers never check the sea or Into the sea, the bottles could of gotten water inside them and sank to the ocean floor, the followers only check on land, but never in the sea. There was a legend that the titanic ship had the lost letters of satan and that people knew about this and rumors said that the titanic hit the iceberg on purpose so nobody would recover it from the ship, the other rumors were that people made a deal with the devil to give him the lost letters but spared there life's in return, that was a rumor I heard from a fellow satanist, but there's to many talks on this subject and nothing has never been recovered, maybe it was a legend or a myth so that we could stay loyal to the dark lord, or maybe it was a game to play to keep us occupied in our daily life's,

I know for a fact that there has been lost letters from satan, there's been to many rumors about this, I believe one day those letters will turned up somewhere, with someone, and I bet that person will have a story to tell all of us, I remember I read in a bible once, and it was vary old, and torn up, but the bible was in Latin, and I knew a little Latin, so I translated the book, and it said that Baphomet has lost his letters and in order to recovery it, you must look into the right spot, and that's were you will find the letters, I never knew what that meant really. But I do know that these rumors are to be true, I just believe people has forgotten about it,

Page 8

In my journey to find the lost letters, I have explore all over the USA, and asked a lot of the satanic members on what they thought about the lost letters, and they told me this, Some people gave me dirty looks and said you were crazy and didn't know what you were talking about, the other people said that they might of heard about satan lost letters, but they thought it was a myth and not true, because they told me that satan is a powerful god, and how would someone like satan could lose such a important letters, I did have a college group say to me that the devils letters were true and that they thought they had a clue to findings these letters, but it was just bad luck, because the clue was a waste of time,

There was one older gentleman that I got spoken to at a bar, at first I didn't know what to believe from this man, but when I got talking to him more, I became hooked In, he would go on telling me that his great, great grandfather was a satanist and that his satanic coven did find one letter that contained a important note about satan, and that it was found inside a broken glass jar, that wash up on the beach, Now do I believe this guy story, we'll to tell you the truth I kinda did but there were flaws into his story, and I had to stay open minded on this and not let it get my hopes up, The man would go on saying that he has this letter at his house and that he would show them to me,

Later that night I would meet this gentleman at his house, and he went by the name Gus, I still felt kinda stupid but I needed to know what he had and to see if it was truly satan hand writings on these old letters, When I sat down on Gus sofa he gave me a big Wooden box and told me to open the box, now at first I was kinda scared to find in this old box but I also felt excited, so when I open the box I saw really old letters that was torn on the sides and it looked like a old vanilla color paper, and it was in Latin, there were just three of this letter, that his great,great grandfather found on the beach, and it did have a hand drawing picture in the middle of the page of Baphomet,

Page 9

But to tell you the truth, most people have not heard about the lost letters of satan, I challenge you all to go up to a satanist and ask him if he has heard any lost letters of satan, I will say he will tell you that you are crazy or doesn't know what you are talking about, I know satan is still upset about loosening the letters, and still angry with himself, But there isn't really much we can do, I know I heard by one of my friends that he read inside a magazine and he said that there was a ship that sunk in the bottom of the sea off the Canadian sea, and divers went down to explore the ship and when they came inside a room, it was a secret room that had crates of bottles and it was clear bottles but he told me he sworn that the bottles had letters inside them,

But don't hold your breath on that one, but that would be awesome if that was true but like I said before I have to stay open minded when I talk to people and listen to there stories, Becuase you just don't know if there stories are true or not, this is why I research this out first, Satan letters contain vary important messages to be added into the bible of satan, this was to complete the bible of satan, I bet you didn't know that the real bible of satan is not complete without the lost letters, this is why satan has been trying to find these letters, to finish his bible, so then we can rejoice about his new book, but unfortunately we will have to wait for that,

There been researchers over a period of time, going inside caves and such, and they think the person who hid the letters most of put them inside a cave, but it's not a 100% accurate! the researcher would say that why they been looking into caves is Because in Colorado state! a miner went into a cave to mine for gold! and blew out a wall that was blocking there way to move forward into the cave! once they got inside the wall they found marking on the wall! and it look like native Americans drawings, but the pictures contain a Indian person building a big fire and a devil looking face surround that fire and the Indian guy holding up a bottle or something close to a bottle! but the drawings on the wall kept on seeing the Indian guy with bottle in his hand! or just a picture of a bottle,

Page 10

The drawings were photograph and cut out of the rock and sent to a Colorado university, but the drawings are real but kept quiet, the drawings were made by the Native American, So I have to wonder if the native Americans had satan lost letters and did they keep it this whole time, I was able to speak with a Native American and ask him if he knew the lost letters of satan, he would tell me that he heard the rumors among his village and that his tribal chief knew something about it, but the tribal chief would not talk to me, but the gentlemen I spoke to said to me, that the devil letters are real and he has saw pictures of Indians with a bottle like shape holding up in the air,

But the gentlemen wasn't for sure if the pictures had any meaning to the lost letters of satan, the pictures I saw look liked a bottle in the hand and people dancing around the fire, I have saw many different native Americans drawings and it always show the same person holding a bottle each time, so I'm thinking the native Americans community knows more then what they are saying, could this tribal group unlock the answers we have been seeking all these years, We'll I say yes to that, it's just not uncommon to see a drawing with a guy dancing around the fire and the fire had a devil looking face inside the fire and the guy holding a bottle up, this tells me that I found a clue and a piece of the puzzle to keep doing my research into this subject?

But it was common for native Americans to draw evil faces inside there drawings to scare the union army and other native Americans tribe away, so it would show bravery and to put fear into the tribes, but I say it can swing both ways, But it's still a mystery today and will be forever, there is someone out there that knows the truth about these letters, they just don't want to give them up, because why turn over these letters, so Christians groups can tear them apart or say a bunch of lies, or could be possibly burn, I believe this is why these letters are in hiding somewhere, I guess something's are just left as a mystery in this world, and no words can explain it,?

Page 11

The letters of satan is true and appear to be real, you have heard the other stories from people that said they have heard this rumors since they were kids, I believe once this mystery is solve, I believe we will really know satan first hand and what he wants from us, I believe that satan is vary real and I know satan gospel is really real, I must say that I will keep searching for the truth of this story, and see if we can unlock the great mystery, I was told that satan is missing roughly about 12 letters and they would be still inside a bottle or inside a book, but were ever it is we should find it,

But I want to share a another letter to you about satan follower and what he said in the letter with satan,

letter 1:

Dear Satan,
I m writing to you to say that I believe the lost letters to be true and real, but I want to know why people have not been looking into the sea and only on the land to be looking, maybe the lost letters is not on land but maybe it's inside the ocean floor somewhere, I will be doing my own research into this and to see if it's to be real, I'm asking for your blessing and protection, while I'm

searching into the sea, I believe the sea is the key to your lost letters, I believe the bottles took under water and sunk to the bottom sea floor, and cover up by the sand, I will be exploring all aspects of this and I hope you can guide me and to help me find your lost letters, I'm your loyal follower & your loyal servant, I will keep you updated along the way my dark lord,a Hail Satan

Sign: Anonymous Person? ..?

Now I was told a big whale wash up on shore because it was bitten by a bigger fish and it died, and when the researchers came to look at it, and get a feel for it, I heard one of the researchers was pushing in the whales belly and heard something like glass banging against something, so the researchers took the dead whale back and did a X-ray on it, but it was never shown to the public or to anyone, it was actually looked up in a safe and about 45 years later it was uncover again,

Page 12

What I was told that the X-Ray showed a glass objects in the whale belly and it looked like paper could have been inside the bottles, but the dead whale was never cut open to see what was in it, the whale really disappeared and to be never found again, So the question is what did the reachers found, did they find satan lost letters inside this bottles, inside the whale, we may never know, this story was a cover up, but what ever it was inside the whale belly must of been something of importance to someone, I've really never heard of a whale just eating anything, but why would a whale have glass objects in it's belly,

I know this is really real, What if I told you that satan was real and that he walked this earth & died on earth, in New Mexico State they have recovered bones that were said to be the devil, and that he was really real, and it was a major biblical findings of the century, I've saw these two photos and let me tell you it gave me goosebumps, it really looked like satan, and it felt just like satan, you can find all the information on google.com and type in New Mexico devil skull. And to to imagines, it's a really cool picture and I'm so happy to found it, because I know now that satan walked this earth and died on this earth as a real human, that is really awesome,

Getting back on track, the devil is in need of someone to find his lost letters, and that if anyone ever found them and called upon satan and said I found your letters, that person would be reward for a life time, and have all the blessings he wanted from satan, and I know satan would make him a lord and a leader inside his kingdom, If you know were these letters are I suggest report it to satan and let him know, but everyday satan is out there on earth just searching his lost letters and just waiting and hopeing to find these letters one day, Like I said before satan lost letters is the key to everything, a key to life, earth, everything we know, is the key roll inside these letters, Like i said before we have the eyewitness and stories from other satanist that said they heard and said the rumors to be true, this wasn't made up at all, this is really the facts, I have been told by satan himself that he lost his letters and that I had to write this book to see if anyone else knew about satans lost letters,

Page 13

In the conclusion of this book, I want to say to you that satan lost letters is true and it's not a myth or a legend, Some of the people I spoke to I was skeptical at first but came to find out that they were speaking from the truth, Some were on this earth, there is satan lost letters, and it's the key to everything, We have heard everything we needed to but I hope you take this book as a research book and a history book, it tells a history about satan and about his lost letters, This has been going on for a vary long time, but it's almost a mystery to me, because all this time we still haven't found the lost letters, or did we find it, I still think it's sitting in someone house be guarded and not being told at all, maybe one day we will unlock this mystery and know the real answers we need to know, I Say onto everyone read this book, please keep a open minded and to stay true to the dark lord,

Not every day you find something new about satan, but I'm determined to find things new about satan, and put it into a book, so you can understand satan more, satan is among us and he's everywhere, and never give up on satan, and thank you for taking the time for reading my book, I hope you enjoyed this book, like I have, Hail Satan, Hail Satan, Hail Satan,

Page 14

A Satanic Group Dedication Page

This satanic book is dedicated to the follow groups, that I share dear to me and how these groups are so awesome, and they are the real deal, but they are also a family group, every member helps another member out, and I've never saw that before, but you can follow these groups on social media, Facebook & Twitter, And we will provide all the information that we have on these groups so you can come to love them to?

The Dark Lords Satanic Group
Founder: Lord Bridges
Email: OurDarkLordSatanicGroup1441@aol.com
Facebook: www.facebook.com/
TheDarkLordsSatanicGroup
Twitter: www.twitter.com/OurSatanicGroup

We offer free membership cards to print out for free, we offer free groups poster & decals, We are a different satanic group and that we are like family, and we are loyal servants to the dark lord, please check us out on social media,

The New Mexico Satanist Group
Founder: Lord Bridges
Email: TheNewMexicoSatanistGroup1441@aol.com
Facebook: www.facebook.com/
TheNewMexicoSatanistGroup
Twitter: www.twitter.com/NMSatainst

This is a brand new group, and these are satanist that want the state of New Mexico as a satanic state, They want to find new members that will join there group and start spreading the word of satan in the community, so if you live in New Mexico and is a satanist this is a group for you to join and support, they are the only satanist group in the state of New Mexico, they are your voice and leader, pretty soon they will start having state conference meetings in Albuquerque, NM once they have a enough members to have the meetings, This group is open to all satanist and please checkout this new group? Hail Satan

I also want to dedicate this book to the defenders of satan group on Facebook for your support in my satanic books and your friendship, Hail Satan

Remember everyone to follow your dreams and to never give up on something you like doing, always stay going and keep on going, until you reach your goals in life,

Page 15

Notes

Notes

Notes

Notes

Notes

Notes

www.ingramcontent.com/pod-product-compliance
Lightning Source LLC
Chambersburg PA
CBHW021920040426
42448CB00007B/839